Mila's Little Book Of Poetry

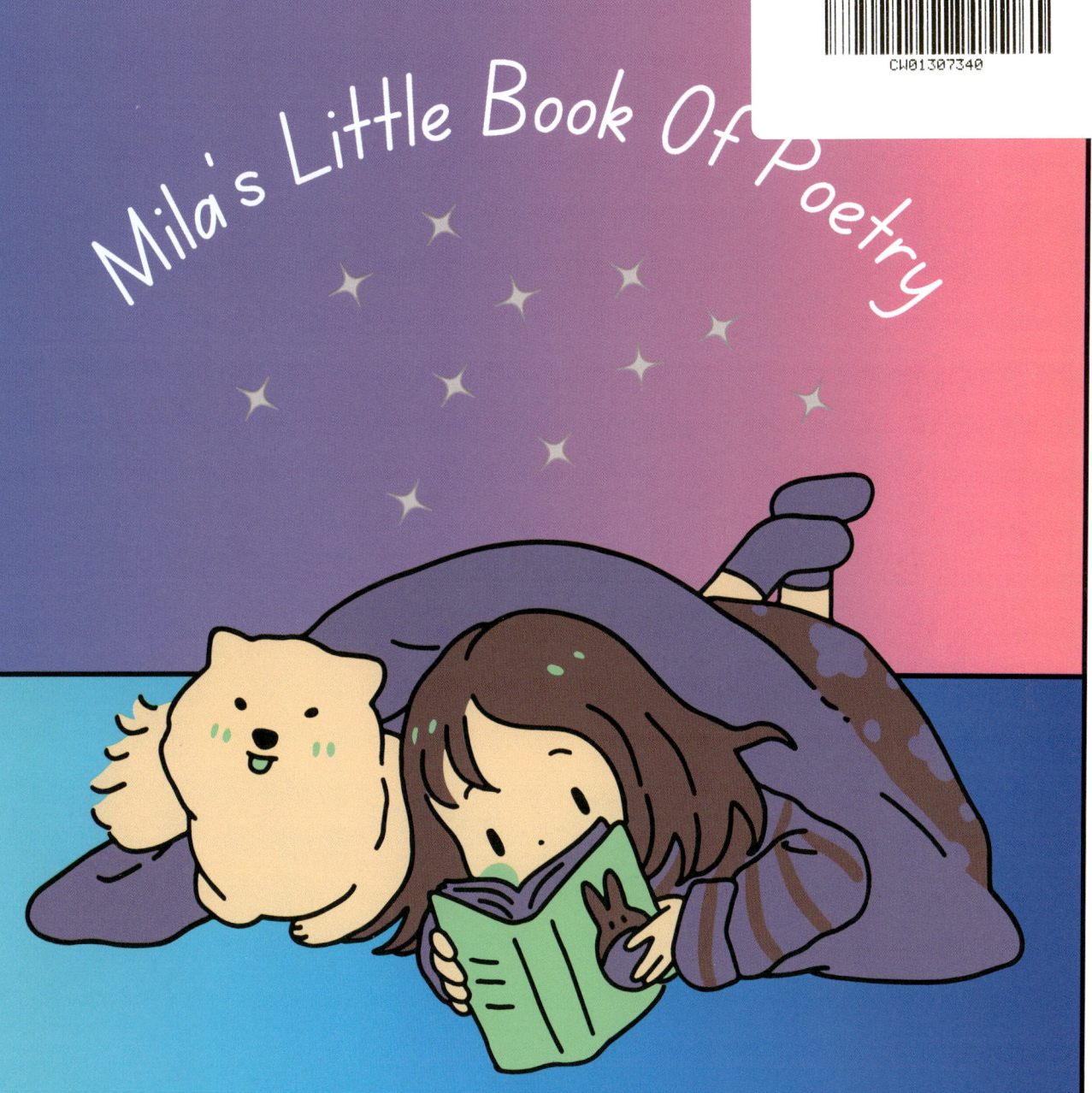

Copyright © Mila Walker 2024
All rights reserved
Mila Walker has asserted her moral right under the
Copyright, Design & Patent Act 1988 and no part of this
work may be reproduced in any way without prior written permission

Cover & Graphics from Canva

Dolphins

Fun little things,
they play a lot,
and lots of teeth,
they have hundreds
that's a lot

their blow hole is big
and out comes squirting water
like an erupting volcano

dolphins are fun
and they always will be

Fantastic Fish

Flappy fins
follow the food
fabulous fellows indeed
fantastic food
they follow

Sand

Soft sand on the beach
soft sand between your feet
soft sand in your hand
soft sand in the sea
soft sand in a bucket
soft sand
everywhere

Roses

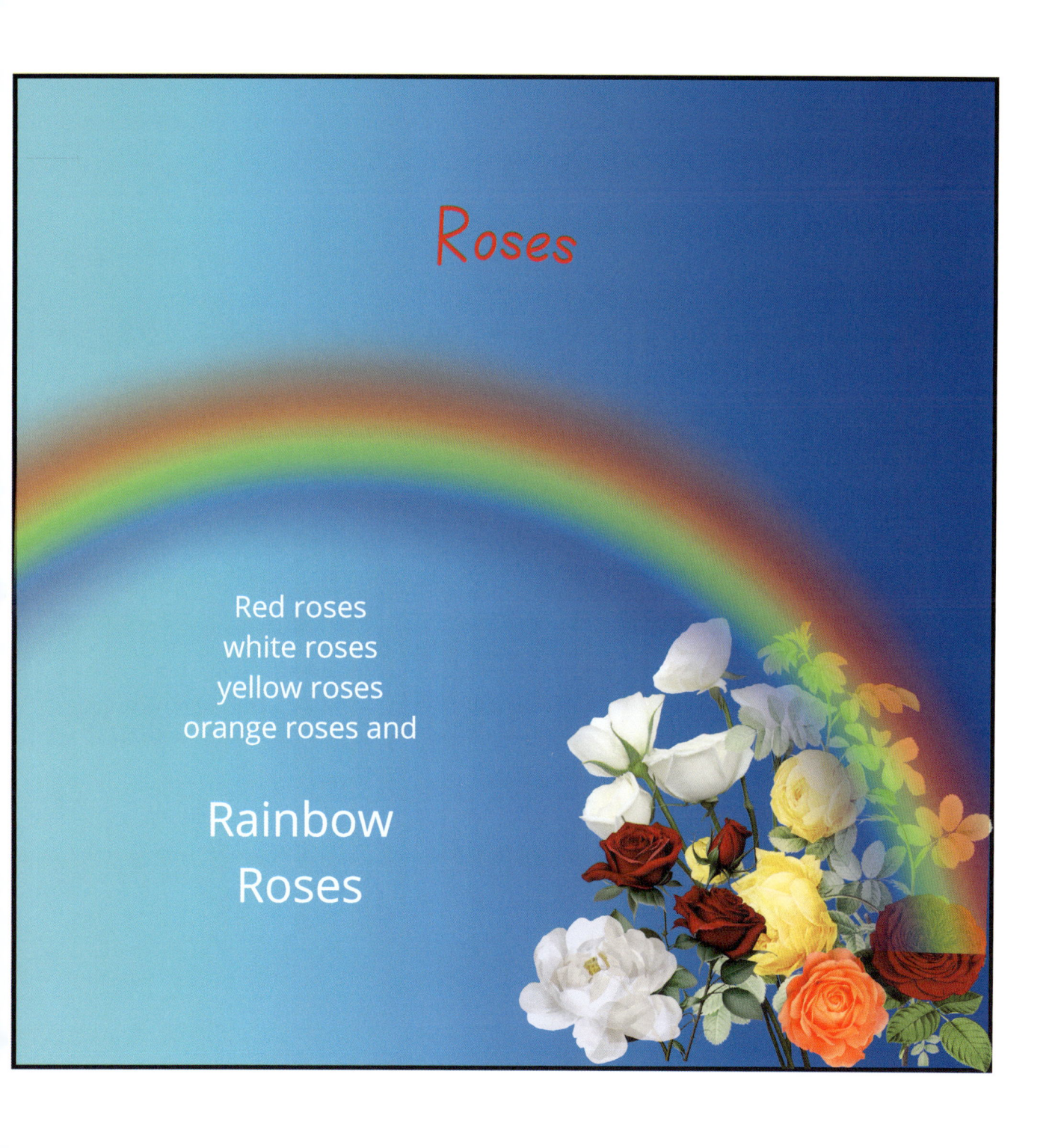

Red roses
white roses
yellow roses
orange roses and

Rainbow Roses

Living

My life is hard
and so is yours
our lives are hard
but they're worth
fighting for

Leaves

Leaves change every season and we change every year

Foxes

Fast fluffy food in the forest

The Night Sky

The night sky
can be dark
but the twinkling stars
will show you
your way home
moon light is the same
as the sun light
but in the dark, dark
side of space
every night I watch and wonder
about the sparkling
moonlit sky

Stones

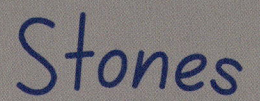

Unique like us
some sparkly gems
some old fossils
that you can
find at the beach

The Only One

Oh lonely star
oh lonely star
where did you come from
because you're the only one
you must be lonely
but the sky will hold you up
and the friendly astronauts
will say hi
the humans will
always love you
if they can see you
so shine bright
just shine bright in the sky
little lonely star

Mischievous

On the floor

Never!

Knowing nothing

Eating fruit

Yeah yummy

Cute
Actually awesome
Terrific ears
Scary to some people

Happiness

Comes and goes
a great feeling did you know
angriness and sadness is ok
but we all prefer
joy and laughter

Trees

Chattering trees
whisper a lot
with no stop
not day or night
and they
keep you awake
all night

Wind

Whisper, whisper
like the wind
it's very calm
but can be
destructive
we like it when
you visit
when we're
a bit hot

Birds

singing a melody
up above
up there flying
in the bright blue sky,
listen and you'll hear them chirping
a brand new song

Bees

bees buzz around with no stop
they buzz to the flowers
and spread the nectar
and finally
my personal favourite they make sweet golden
HONEY

Fireworks

Loud, big and look pretty colourful like a dandelion

Families

You don't have to be
related to be family like
me and my class were
family you can be family
with your friends
or neighbours
and maybe
even your community
like
these two kids

Fun!
Racers
Omnivores
Great at hopping

Colours

They're everywhere
here and there
inside outside
turquoise is my favourite
what is yours?

Art

Art can be anything
not just drawing and
painting
it could be photos
and even how you
place some twigs and
leaves
art can express your
feelings in many
different ways

sailing

We're sailing across the big blue sea avoiding the pirates Aarghhh me hearty quick, they're here! run, run, RUN!

All about the Author

My name is Mila,
I am eight years old, I'm home educated.
I love nature, space and the sea.
My true passion is art and my full name is
Mila Aveline Walker.
I started writing poems at the age of six
and created this book to express my
feelings and give my poetry to the world.

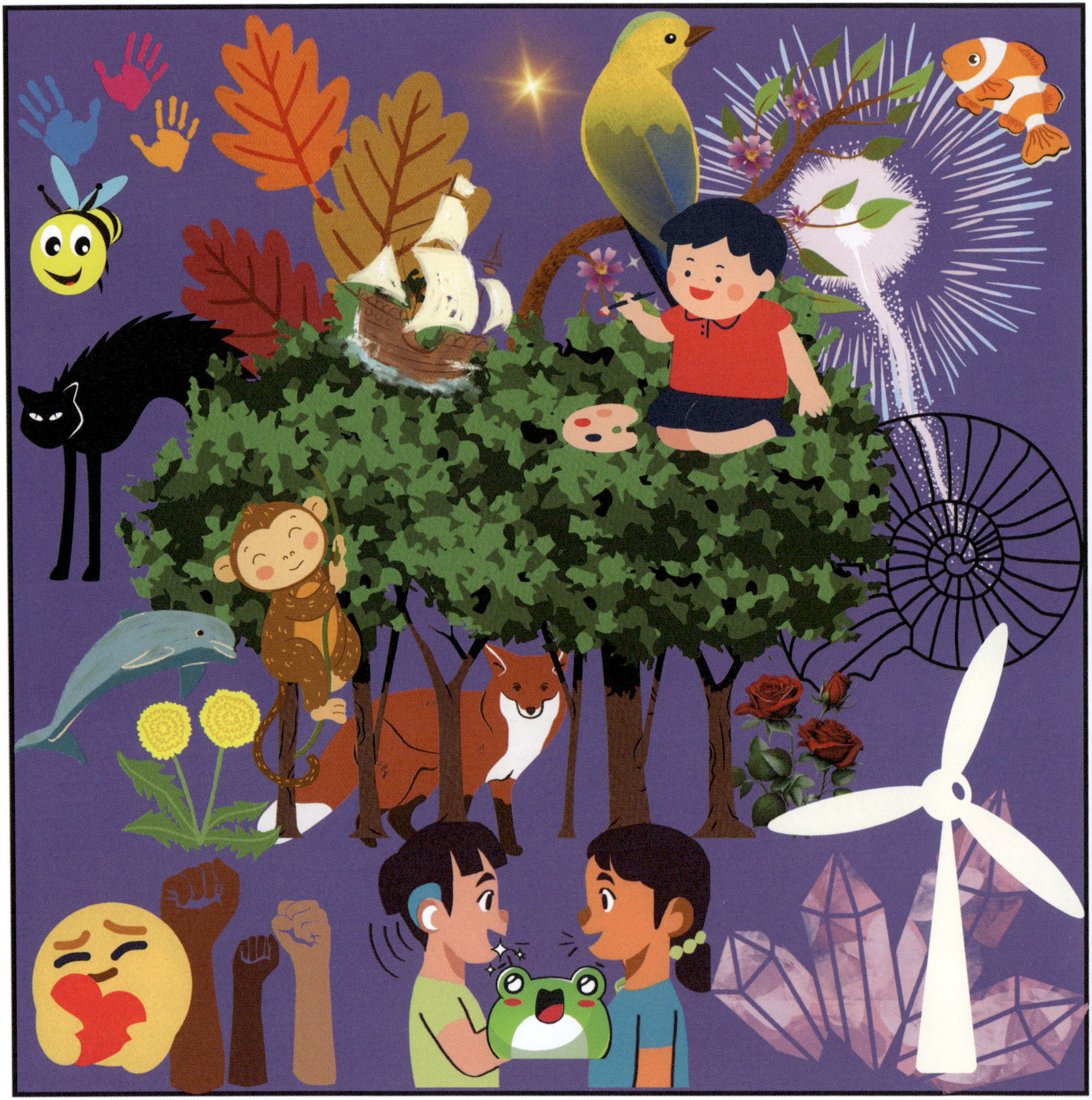

Printed in Great Britain
by Amazon